Resurrecting Abel: A Discourse on Brotherly Love

Resurrecting Abel: A Discourse on Brotherly Love

Marcus M. Johnson, Jr.

Printed in the United States of America

ISBN: 978-1541332133

Author and book inquiries should be directed to the following:

Nickel Bag Books
925 Main Street
Suite 100-30
Stone Mountain, Georgia 30083
nickelbagbooks@gmail.com

Table of Contents

Part I: The Death

"Everyone who hates his brother is a murderer, and you know that no murderer has eternal life abiding in him."

- 1 John 3:15

1
Fratricide

The inundation of the market with cellphones that are equipped with cameras and video technology has led to an increase in violent acts being caught on film. In most cases, offenders are held responsible. However, in cases that involve Blue-On-Black violence (police brutality directed toward Black people), instances of arrests, trials, and convictions are underwhelming. A lack of satisfaction with police and white men getting away with killing members of the Black community has resulted in demonstrations and protests, all over the world.

Dissatisfaction with the failure to hold people accountable for what appears to be an attack on Blackness has led to the emergence of groups that include Black Lives Matter, and chants and hashtags that include #ICantBreathe and #HandsUpDontShoot. Reactions to the perceived injustice have not always remained peaceful and have in some cases resulted in the disruption of events, destruction of commercial property, and more loss of life.

Rebuttals from those who find protests and demonstrations calling for an acknowledgement and revaluation of Black people in America have ranged from shrugs to reciprocated violence and protests. One inappropriate response that has been regularly used is that which seeks to redirect attention from unpunished crimes against Black people by non-Black people to Black-On-Black crimes. There are several reasons that make this particular invocation inappropriate. First, Black-On-Black crime is only slightly more prevalent than other ethnicities' crimes against themselves. These phenomena are easily explained by the fact that people have a tendency to congregate and live in communities that are populated by people with whom they identify. White people live among each other, Hispanics around Hispanics, Latinos around Latinos, etc. As a result, the probability of being victimized by one of your own is increased. Now that we have addressed this, let us deal with that elephant in the room, Black-On-Black violence.

Black-On-Black violence is a topic that is only around to be thrown in the face of the Black community because we have failed to effectively address it. The first step toward addressing it, is to call it what it is, fratricide. Fratricide is a term that is most-commonly used to describe military occurrences of friendly fire that end in loss of life. These occurrences are typically viewed as accidental or unintentional. A broader definition of the word that relates to civilians defines the term as an instance of killing one's brother or sister. This is exactly what Black-On-Black violence is, fratricide.

Fratricide is neither unique to the Black community nor a new development in World History. There is no shortage of cultural myths or religious narratives that chronicle fratricides and with which most of us are familiar. Examples of fratricide are connected to nearly every continent.

From Europe, there are the twin founders of Rome, Remus and Romulus. These two agreed to establish a city, but not on the location. Remus wanted to found the city upon Aventine Hill, while Romulus favored building it upon Palatine Hill. Unable to settle this difference of opinion, the two willingly participate in a contest which favored Remus. Unable to accept this, Romulus eventually kills Remus, and founds the city, naming it after himself.

From Africa, we have the Egyptian tale of Osiris and Set. Legend says that these two were children of Geb, the god of the sky, and Nut, goddess of the earth. As a result of a curse, Nut should not have been able to bare children but bore many, including these two. Osiris grew to be respected by most and this was the source of what some call the jealously of Set. The story goes on to tell of Set transforming himself into some sort of monster, killing Osiris, mutilating the body of his murdered brother, and distributing the pieces all across Egypt. It was the love of Osiris's sisters – one of which being his wife Isis – that led to his body being reassembled and his resurrection.

Perhaps the biggest collection of fratricides and sibling conflicts is found in the Holy Bible. One story is of Amnon and Absalom. Amnon was in love with his sister Tamar and eventually raped her, as a result of his unchecked lust. To avenge what Amnon did to their sister, Absalom kills Amnon. Other tales of fraternal conflict in the Bible include Jacob taking Esau's birthright and Joseph who was sold into slavery by his brothers. Perhaps the most famous Biblical fratricide, the first according to Biblical history, is when Cain killed Abel.

Many siblings, although they may come from the same mother and/or father, are unique individuals. The same holds true for Cain and Abel. Abel was a herdsman who kept flocks of domesticated animals, while Cain was more of a horticulturalist who worked the land, harvesting crops. The narrative tells of how both of the brothers made offerings to the Lord from the fruits of their labor. However, it appeared that the Lord was more pleased with the offerings of Abel. This disturbed Cain. As a result of his discontent, Cain lured Abel to the field, where he committed the first murder. As a result of his crime against brother, God forbade anyone to kill Cain, marked him to make sure that it did not happen, and Cain was exiled from the Lord's presence.

The example of Cain and Abel is important, not simply because it is a Bible narrative but because it looks at the type of animosity that leads to fratricide, sibling rivalry born of not seeing how everyone's role is connected and important in its own right. The Cain and Abel narrative also illustrates how fratricide has an effect on both the victim and the victimizer, a multi-dimensional effect that we continue to see adversely affecting the Black community.

The Black community has been made vulnerable to destructive criticism and concrete harm from without by unresolved issues from within. It is beyond time for the discussion on fratricide and time to plan for the reversal of generations of loveless interactions between Black men, in particular. It is time to begin resurrecting Abel.

2

My Brother

There is no one for whom fratricide should not be a concern. Many who read this book may say to themselves, "I am an only child" or "I have sisters." However, there must be an acknowledgement of the broader definition of brotherhood, especially within the Black community. *Green's Dictionary of Slang* (2010) notes fifteen uses of the term "brother," six of which are from African American Vernacular English (AAVE). The six uses are predominately terms of endearment and date as far back as the early 20th Century. The term is used as a term of identification of Black men by Black men, as well as by white men. It also has a history of being used to identify non-Black men who have been accepted by the black community. It is a term that underscores and reinforces the bond between Black men.

Since the 1960s, the use of "brother" has been gradually replaced with the word "nigger." *Green's Dictionary of Slang* (2010) has 119 different uses and definitions of "nigger," the majority and earliest of which are derogatory. The word has both positive and negative uses in AAVE. However, it is more likely that you would hear a Black man call another Black man "nigger" than "brother." Why is this problematic?

"Brother" is a term that has always been used to show kinship and solidarity. Kinship and solidarity is particularly important to the Americanized Africans who have been struggling to self-determine after generations removed from their native lands and under one of worst, if the not the most egregious, forms a chattel slavery recorded in World History.

American chattel slavery should never be forgotten or "gotten over." However, we can move beyond allowing it to be a psychosocial shackle. Remembering what we have overcome can be used as a tool to promote unity and encourage pursuit of greatness. Before this shift can occur, Black people have to neutralize the active components of that system and discard them. Those components include the harmful vocabulary, which is intertwined with many toxic elements that complicate vital relationships, like those between Black men. We are brothers and owe each other nothing less than the respect of properly recognizing each other as such.

3

Where is the Love?

How many black men and boys did you walk past without greeting, today? To some, lack of acknowledgement or greeting is a non-entity; however, it is really a symptom of a greater issue. Because we greet and acknowledge those for whom we have respect and love, the lack thereof indicates a deficiency. This deficiency in Black men's interactions with one another is best described as a lack of fraternal love. Where has the love that held Black men together for generations gone?

In the Sciences, there are agents that are described as inhibitors. These inhibitors are so called because they have a relationship with some other agent, in which they decrease the effectiveness of that other agent. Black fraternal love has its own inhibitors. Lack of fraternal love between Black men can be attributed to many things, including competition, homophobia, and internalized self-hatred.

One factor that creates division and obstructs Black men's ability to love one another is competition. Not all competition is negative. In sports and academia, friendly competition can encourage competitors to work harder and excel. In sports, some of the greatest rivalries have led to the greatest performances. Where would Michael Jordan be had his performances not been driven by Magic Johnson, Larry Bird, and others? Academic competition has a similar effect. In academia, we can find cases where competition can lead to excellence and help combat mediocrity and underachievement.

There are, however, arenas in which competition is unhealthy and even fatal. Not every sphere of life is an appropriate arena for competition. Instances of unhealthy competition can be found in territorial struggles that are shaped by primitive desires to conquer. The animalistic need to feel dominate and be the Alpha male, although not unique to Black masculinity, is an issue that is often manifested in fraternal violence. Think about some of the principles that drive gang involvement and activity. In addition to the unhealthy varieties of competition, homophobia is another factor that obstructs fraternal love between Black men.

Understanding the connection between homophobia and the lack of love requires at least a brief note on "guilt by association." "Guilt by association" is a term that is used in many ways. In one use, it applies to philosophies and objects. For example, the Bible has been misused by bad people and has been consequently viewed as bad by some groups of people. Another example can be found in some people's thoughts on guns. For some, guns are bad because they have been misused. Another application of guilt by association involves people.

Most are familiar with the saying "birds of a feather flock together." This application of guilt by association is one in which people are assumed to be like the people with whom they associate. This can be good and bad. People thinking that you are a kind person because you are often in the company of kind people can have its advantages. On the other hand, police assuming that you are a criminal because you have friends who are associated with crime can put you at a disadvantage and in real danger.

Not all Black men are gay, and men living double-lives to hide homosexual tendencies is not a phenomenon that exists only within the Black community. However, because of historically hostile attitudes toward homosexuals in minority communities, there are many who hide their sexual preferences. This leads to a lot of guessing and accusations. No one wants to be exposed and made vulnerable. At the same time, no one wants to be mislabeled. As a result, at least two attempts to disassociate with homosexuality can be found among heterosexual men, hyper-sexuality and the inability to show physical affection.

As someone who regularly attends church functions, this is something that I can say is regularly observable there, from the restrooms to the sanctuaries. Many men are afraid to speak to each other, beyond the sinks. Even though the bathroom is not exactly the place for meetings, there is a noticeable tension there. In interactive churches, where parishioners are instructed to do things like hold your neighbor's hand or hug your neighbor, discomfort with physical contact between men can also be seen. This is not an absolute, but it is too common an occurrence to not be spoken on. It should be difficult to not make the connection between homophobia and the inability to do something so simple as hold hands or hug.

Great strides are being made in father-son relationships; however, this has historically been another area in which homophobia obstructs expressions or demonstrations of love. How many boys have grown up without a memory of being kissed or hugged regularly by their fathers or grandfathers? Father-son relationships can be viewed as ground zero for the stigmatization of expressed and demonstrated love between Black men. There is a fear that is rooted in fallacy and needs to be eradicated. Fraternal love is not gay! It is human! The stigmatization of fraternal love can lead to self-hatred.

Self-hatred, like guilt by association, has many forms. One form of self-hatred involves a person actually hating themselves. Another form, the one that is most-important to this discourse, involves hating people like you. There are several plausible root causes for this self-hatred. Perhaps the most plausible is the fact that the Black American experience is not monolithic. I cannot take credit for this statement. It is actually something that I was inspired to consider by an episode of *Lincoln Heights*, a family television series that aired on ABC for roughly two years. The show dealt with a middle-class Black family that moved into a rough Black neighborhood and had trouble fitting in. Taylor Sutton, also known as "Tay," experienced bullying and was indicted by other neighborhood boys as not being Black enough. In response to this, his mother explained to him that Blackness comes in many forms. This is important because it highlights what has eroded the collective conscious of the Black community.

In *Disintegration: The Splintering of Black America* (2010), author Eugene Robinson further explores the varieties of Black Americans. Robinson places Black Americans into four classes. These four classes include the abandoned poor, immigrants and racially-mixed individuals, the middle class, and the elite. Some have not been and will not be able to appreciate Robinson's work and will dismiss it as a generalization. While it does generalize Blackness, it is in an effort to better understand Blackness and free people from the constraints of the broader generalization that is the catalyst of racism and prejudice. The most valuable aspect of his work is that he identifies how society has allowed the evolution of Blackness along several different tracks. Unfortunately, these different tracks mean that the community is very splintered, a phenomenon that an oppressed community cannot afford. There is not always the opportunity to move between these different groups and this leads to malice, etc.

The whole world is experiencing a love deficiency. Zooming in on the demographic of which I am a part, reveals certain culprits for the love deficiency between Black men. One obstacle that obstructs this love is unreasonable competition. Another is homophobia. A third obstacle that interferes with Black fraternal love is the diminished collective conscious, which has been aided by limited opportunities for upward social mobility, desegregation, integration, and the overall fragmentation and dispersing of our country's older minority communities. Black men may or may not be able to contribute to fixing the global love deficiency; however, we definitely have the ability to remove the obstacles that obstruct our ability to love one another.

Part II: The Resurrection

"And above all things have fervent charity among yourselves: for charity shall cover the multitude of sins."

- 1 Peter 4:8 KJV

The root cause of Black men's inability to love each other is an amalgam of the sins of many different groups of people; however, the failure to take control of the situation is mostly our fault. We have continued to float along, being victimized by the conditions, not doing enough to change them. This section proposes that we adopt the following habits to right the ship and change course: acknowledgement, validation, encouragement, and articulation and demonstration of love. Some already do these things. These things may not result in the immediate demolition of all of our obstacles; however, they can put us on a track toward resurrecting Abel and reversing an ugly, self-destructive tradition.

4

Acknowledge Thy Brother

The first step toward resurrecting Abel is for Black men to acknowledge one another. Acknowledgement is an action that we must understand the significance of and intentionally practice. *The Merriam-Webster Dictionary* provides four definitions for "acknowledge." The first definition says, "to recognize the rights, authority, or status of." The second entry defines it as "to disclose knowledge of or agreement with." Next, it is defined as "to express gratitude or obligation for," "to take notice of," or "to make known the receipt of." Lastly, it is defined as "to recognize as genuine or valid" ("Acknowledge"). Our acknowledgement of each other should be characterized by all of the above definitions.

Black men have to begin recognizing the rights, authority, or status of one another, or the lack thereof. How do we recognize the rights, authority, or status of one another? To recognize the rights of one another, we must first know what those rights are. I do not expect you to be able to rattle off every local, state, and federal law, at the drop of a hat. This may be a future goal. For now, we can make sure that the rights that we are aware of are not being violated. When we do recognize the rights of one of our brothers being trample upon, we should feel obligated to intercede in a lawful manner, even if this means gently letting each other know when we are in the wrong. In addition to recognizing and defending the rights of one another, we need to recognize the authority of one another.

While none of us have absolute authority that transcends all boundaries, every man has a place where he has authority. Examples of this include our property and our bodies. When we are on one of our brothers' properties, we need to show him the highest respect by not abusing his property, this includes homes and cars. Authority also extends to interactions with family units. We often see people interacting with their children and spouses, or even handling themselves in ways with which we may not agree. If no religious laws or laws of the land are being broken, we may offer our views if an appropriate opportunity presents itself, but we must ultimately respect the authority figure.

One of the above definitions of acknowledge involves the expression of gratitude. We do not always have the opportunity to do this; however, we should be more sensitive to opportunities to express gratitude in our brother-to-brother interactions than in any other interactions. Every time a brother holds the door for you, offers to help, lets you cut into traffic, etc., there should be a clear response of gratitude.

Acknowledgment is nothing, if not practiced. Take a week and record how many times you acknowledge a brother, as defined above. See if you can increase it, daily. Keep practicing, until this becomes habit.

5

Validate Thy Brother

In addition to acknowledging one another, Black men must also consciously validate one another. Think of the last time that you visited somewhere that required payment for parking. Now, think of the last time that you parked in a paid parking deck or lot but did not have to pay because the place that you were visiting validated your parking. What did that parking validation really mean? Hopefully, you realized that it acknowledged your presence in that parking deck for an acceptable reason. Acknowledgement and validation overlap. Although the *Merriam-Webster Dictionary* has at least five definitions for "validate," this text is going to focus on the definition that says, "to recognize, establish, or illustrate the worthiness or legitimacy of" ("Validate").

Although our presence is contested and leads to threats in many places, we are all here for a reason, and our presence means something. This does not mean that we should revert to a state of existence where we feel less valuable if we are not validated by someone. It is more about re-establishing and maintaining a stronger collective.

Recognizing each other is as simple as greeting one another. We should be greeting every single human being that we encounter. However, if we do not do that, the least we as Black men should do is greet every Black man and boy that we encounter. It is important that we see, know that we are seen by each other, and find comfort in viewing and being seen. Early in her book *Post Traumatic Slave Syndrome* (2005), author Dr. Joy DeGruy introduces a concerning dichotomy between Africans and Black people in America.

The dichotomy is found in how Black people in America respond to being looked at versus their African brothers' responses to the same exchanges. Dr. DeGruy notes that this is a source of discomfort for Black Americans. In contrast, she writes how she not only witnessed people throughout Africa looking at each other and allowing themselves to be viewed, but also utilizing greetings that literally meant "I see you." We have to get to this level of comfort with one another, in America. This is acknowledgment and validation. It is likely that the discomfort in being viewed by one another has grown out of being viewed and looking at one another and failing to verbally greet one another. Let us reunify the parts of meaningful greetings. Look and speak.

Just as the Acknowledge section had a challenge, the Validate section has one. Take a week, preferably after the Acknowledge week, and verbally validate as many Black men you can, keeping track of it, and trying to improve your numbers, daily. Acknowledging is as simple as a head nod, but you are going to have to open your mouth to meet the expectations of the Validation challenge. Do not just nod and say "Hi" or "What's up." Ask how a few of your brothers are doing. Let them know that you see them and care about them. The level of caring that you demonstrate through acknowledging and validating your brothers helps build relationships that are favorable for effective encouragement.

6

Encourage Thy Brother

Encouragement is an incredible thing. It effects people positively and negatively, can come from within or without, and covers nearly every industry. While searching for the most accurate terminology to describe the spectacle that can be witnessed in sports, churches, etc., an article on Simply Psychology's website surfaced. Saul McLeod's 2011 article "Social Facilitation" covers a phenomenon that many of us may identify as a form of social or peer pressure.

In the article, named after the concept that it covers, McLeod defines "social facilitation" as "an improvement in performance produced by the mere presence of others" (McLeod). He goes on to establish co-action and audience effects as the two types of social facilitation. The co-action effect is driven by the presence of individuals who are performing the same task. Imagine a runner that is not the fastest but out-performs his- or herself when running in the company of other runners. The other type of social facilitation, audience effect, does not require someone to participate in the action with the performer, but the performance is affected by just having an audience. To get a better grasp of this concept, imagine a high school basketball player who over- or underperforms, as a result of his or her awareness of a college scout in the audience or a musician who kicks their performance up a notch because of the presence of a competitor or critique. Encouragement can be both of these forms of social facilitation and it is because of this that we need to understand it and use it effectively to edify and support our brothers.

When we see brothers excelling, we need to salute them and encourage them. Even if they are not quite meeting their objectives and we see them making visible efforts, we should encourage them. Too often, we remember mistakes and back when people were living unsavory lifestyles. We are quick to breathe new life into those old narratives, even when the subject may have moved in a completely different direction. We need to be as adamant and determined in our identification and measurement of positive growth. Use encouragement and social facilitation to propel someone farther in the right direction or to make them change directions for the better.

For a week that does not coincide with your initial Acknowledge or Validate challenges, pursue an Encouragement challenge, during which you seize every opportunity to encourage your fellow Black men. Increase those efforts, each day of the challenge.

7

Articulate & Demonstrate Love for Thy Brother

Raise your hand, if you have ever had a night of imbibing with friends that ended with a sloppy round of hugs and I-Love-You's. There is something about alcohol that makes these expressions so easy, especially among the guys who otherwise experience difficulty with expressions and displays of fraternal love. Outpourings of fraternal love are also commonly found around sickbeds and at funerals. Sorrow also makes it easy to be vocal and honest about feelings. There are adages for both of these instances, including one of my favorites which says "A drunk man's words are a sober man's thoughts." Why do we have to be intoxicated or heartbroken to say or show how we really feel?

On his album *Be* (2005), Common has a song called "Love Is" in which he says, "As men we were taught to hold it in/That's why we don't know how 'til we're older men" (Lynn et al). We live in a sexist society that has assigned gender to emotions. Consequently, in an attempt to live up to a sexist model of masculinity, we have adopted a model that is causing us harm. It is like being given a blood transfusion with a blood type that neither matches your own nor is universal. Such a transfusion will cause your immune system to react in a way that is possibly fatal. Black men are experiencing a similar effect with their adoption of a loveless version of masculinity that is neither universal nor a match for us. Treatment of this self-induced harm is theoretically as simple as unplugging the IV (intravenous cord) and turning toward a model of masculinity that involves telling our brothers that we love them and showing it.

Hopefully, each person who reads this book will be able to nod and testify to the power of someone telling them that they love them. Love has the ability to motivate people to do good and bad beyond what they could ever imagine. Throughout my lifetime, there have been countless tales of mother and fathers lifting cars off of their children, feats that some attribute to extreme stress and others to hysterical love. There have also been horrible things, like men killing women's husbands because of misguided love. Whether good or bad, love – a form of eustress – can motivate people to exceed limitations and obstacles. Every demographic is faced with some sort of obstacle or limitation that is the result of uncontrollable conditions. As Black men in America – a place which at its height was the crown jewel of White Supremacist Capitalist Patriarchy – we represent the absolute antithesis of what the country was intended to be. As a result, there are obstacles between us and everything that is considered a worthy goal by American standards. With such an extreme course of obstacles and booby-traps, we need something to motivate us to supernatural strengths. That something is fraternal or brotherly love. We need to be bold enough to tell our brothers that we love them and show them.

The articulation and demonstration of love is most-effective when used as a supplement. It needs to be used as a supplement for our acknowledgement, validation, and encouragement of our brothers. When we supplement these with articulation and demonstration of love, our acknowledgement will begin to incorporate handshakes, open-hand dap, and eventually embraces. Our validation will evolve from simple expressions to acts that show that we appreciate one another's presence. Our encouragement will evolve into the reversal of the Crab Mentality that prevents some from celebrating the success of others and will grow into feelings of personal success when one of our brothers succeeds at any level.

After you have completed the other challenges that have been set forth, combine all them with articulations and demonstrations of love and make it more than a week- or month-long challenge. Make it a habit. It is time for us to make a sober man's thoughts his sober words and actions. It is time to stop holding love in, until it is too late. Brothers, we need this love.

Part III: The Possibility

8
Conclusion

Black men have enough to worry about, including combating negative stereotypes, and re-establishing and/or maintaining roles as positive contributors to family units and in the various levels of our communities. These things are, in many cases, contingent upon factors that are beyond our control, like employment with livable wages and overcoming prejudices. The last thing that we need to add to our plates is disharmony with others who are experiencing the same struggles.

The lack of unity among Black men is poison in a well upon which the entire Black community is dependent. It leads to issues with our female counterparts and our children. It perpetuates the cycle of poor treatment due to stereotypes. It is our responsibility to identify the root causes and work diligently to overcome and break this destructive cycle.

We can sit around and continue to say that this is just how it is or we can talk about the causes noted above (unhealthy competition, homophobia, and internalized self-hatred), or the many other causes, and take action. We cannot change the past but I charge Black men in America to change the future by incorporating acknowledgement, validation, encouragement, and demonstration and articulation of love in our interactions with other Black men.

Toni Morrison's *Beloved* (1987) is a piece of art that paints a portrait of how our real narrative can end. *Beloved* is a tragic tale of relationships that are haunted and destroyed by an unresolved past. The story includes infanticide, and broken filial and romantic relationships. The final resolution of the story comes when the women of the community stop vilifying Sethe, the stories main protagonist, and unify to expel the ghost of the chattel slavery that has driven the dysfunction in Sethe's life. It is a case of women coming together to liberate a woman. Men, our story is this story. We have simply replaced infanticide with fratricide. The ghost that haunts us, like Sethe's antagonist, will only be defeated by our love for one another.

Bibliography

"Acknowledge." *Merriam-Webster.com*. Merriam-Webster, n.d. Web. 27 Dec. 2016.

"Brother." *Green's Dictionary of Slang*. Chambers, 2010. https://greensdictofslang.com/search/basic?q=brother. Accessed 28 Dec. 2016.

DeGruy, Joy. *Post Traumatic Slave Syndrome: America's Legacy of Enduring Injury and Healing*. Uptone Press, 2005.

King James Version. Bible Gateway. Web. 29 Dec. 2016.

Lynn, Lonnie, et al. "Love Is." 2005. By Common. *Be*. Geffen Records, 2005. CD.

"Manchild." *Lincoln Heights: The Complete First Season*, written by Yolanda Lawrence, directed by Bobby Roth, ABC Family, 2007.

McLeod, S. A. (2011). Social Facilitation. Retrieved from www.simplypsychology.org/Social-Facilitation.html

Morrison, Toni. *Beloved*. Knopf, 1987.

"Nigger." *Green's Dictionary of Slang*. Chambers, 2010. https://greensdictofslang.com/entry/n52s6ey. Accessed 28 Dec. 2016

Robinson, Eugene. *Disintegration Nation: The Splintering of Black America*. Doubleday, 2010.

"Validate." *Merriam-Webster.com*. Merriam-Webster, n.d. Web. 27 Dec. 2016.

Author Bio

Marcus M. Johnson, Jr. is a collegiate English instructor, writer, consultant, and mentor to at-risk youth. In addition to these roles, he is also a dedicated worker within his religious community.

Other works by Marcus include *Concentrated Blackness: An Inward-looking Solution to the Plight Americanized Africans* (2016).

www.ingramcontent.com/pod-product-compliance
Lightning Source LLC
Chambersburg PA
CBHW070232290526
45789CB00004B/1586